The Phantom Frog

by Irene Belnik
illustrated by Kersti Frigell

Core Decodable 88

McGraw Hill Education

Bothell, WA • Chicago, IL • Columbus, OH • New York, NY

MHEonline.com

Send all inquiries to:
McGraw-Hill Education
8787 Orion Place
Columbus, OH 43240

ISBN: 978-0-02-143401-5
MHID: 0-02-143401-8

Printed in Canada.

9 10 11 12 KOD 24

Phillip and Ralph take a hike.
They left their cell phones at home.

Phillip finds leaves like elephant ears.
Ralph takes photographs of birds.

Peep, peep, peep.
"Think that's a gopher?" asks Ralph.
Phillip whispers, "Maybe it's a phantom!"

"Don't be silly!" scolds Ralph. "Phantoms are phony."

Peep, peep, peep.

"Then what is it?" asks Phillip.

Phillip looks for phantoms.

Ralph whispers, "Wait. Let me take a photo of this frog."

Peep, peep, peep.

"I see the phantom. It's the little frog," Ralph tells Phillip.